SECRETS *of the* PERMAFREE BOOK

HOW TO PUBLISH A FREE BOOK ON AMAZON

DALE L. ROBERTS

Secrets of the Permafree Book: How to Publish a Free Book on Amazon

Second edition ©2020

Originally published as *Secrets to the Permafree Book: A Step-by-Step Guide on How to Drastically Improve Your Self-Publishing Business in Six Months or Less*

First edition ©2016 One Jacked Monkey, LLC

All rights reserved. February 25, 2016.

No part of this book may be reproduced or transmitted in any form or by any means, electronic or mechanical, including photocopying, recording or by any information storage and retrieval system, without the permission in writing from the author.

Disclaimer

Although the author has made every effort to ensure that the information in this book was correct at press time, the author does not assume and hereby disclaims any liability to any party for any loss, damage, or disruption caused by errors or omissions, whether such errors or omissions result from negligence, accident, or any other cause.

Publishing services provided by

ISBN: 978-1-950043-17-0

So you're ready to launch your book?

I bet you want the best book launch possible.

Of course you do!

What if you could increase your odds of hitting the Bestsellers List in your niche?

Download a copy of my
Bestseller Book Launch Checklist…

Go, sign up!

DaleLinks.com/Checklist

Start your action plan to a better book launch right now!

CONTENTS

Introduction 1

Chapter 1: Creating a Multipurpose Book 3

Chapter 2: Building an Email List 8

Chapter 3: The Ideal Permafree Book 13

Chapter 4: The Back Door to Large Online Retailers ... 16

Chapter 5: Fully Utilize Your Free Content 22

Conclusion 24

A Small Ask… 26

About the Author 27

INTRODUCTION

Early in my publishing career, I discovered something rather interesting. While I put my books on a 5-day free promotion through the KDP Select program, I found other books doing the same. These other books shared the same category as mine, had practically the same content, yet had something distinguishably different from mine. The publications were permanently free.

Perplexed by this discovery, I dug deeper to find these books did not share the same availability as mine. First, they were not enrolled in the KDP Select program. Next, they were available for free in other major online retailers (i.e. Apple, Barnes & Noble, etc.). Finally, Amazon doesn't allow books to be priced below $0.99, so how were these publishers getting away with this price hack?

Quite simply, these publishers found if they made their content available free on other major online retailers, then Amazon would price match their competition. But, the issues for me were:

1. Why would anyone make content available for free?

2. How did they do it?

3. Was doing this practice against Amazon policy?

Self-publishing insiders call these books, permafree, or permanently free. With a little research and some practice, I found this process was simple to do, accepted by Amazon, and helped build a brand. In fact, after publishing over a dozen permafree books, I saw my self-publishing business explode, and my residual income expand exponentially. However, it was not without making a few mistakes along the way and employing strategies of successful self-publishing entrepreneurs. Let's dig in!

CHAPTER 1
CREATING A MULTIPURPOSE BOOK

Most people want to know why a self-publisher would go through the effort to produce a quality book only to release it for free on multiple online retailers. After all, wouldn't these permafree books have more perceived value and gain more wealth in the long run with a minimal cost? This question is sound and makes even more sense if an author releases hack work.

ADVERTISE & ESTABLISH BRAND PRESENCE

Permafree books are perfect for essentially advertising at no cost. Unless you contract a freelance writer to produce content, a permafree book only requires a small investment, a little time, and the same deliberate steps of a normal publication.

Much like any decent-performing book, your publication should have these four fundamentals:

1. An attractive cover

2. An enticing book description

3. Valuable, well-written content

4. Optional: A keyword-rich title and/or subtitle

If your permafree book doesn't have these critical elements, then no amount of a price reduction will direct the ideal audience to you. And, reader engagement is ultimately what you want when producing a permafree book. So, master the previously mentioned fundamentals of self-publishing to get the most from your permafree books.

Once your book is free on all online retailers, you will see an uptick in attention and reader engagement. Essentially, the book works as a free advertisement for you and your brand. Also, the free books act as a gateway to your normally-priced books. Once you have two to four flagship publications and about six to eight permafree books, your customers have an unending supply of content. With eight to twelve books for your readers to choose, you have established a solid foundation and a strong brand presence.

BUILD VALUE & GAIN CREDIBILITY AS AN AUTHORITY

Providing a quality publication at no cost establishes a platform to showcase your abilities or expertise. Then, the readers who picked up your book at no cost begin to view you as an authority in your niche or subject.

So, if you write books on the benefits of herbal remedies, then your readers will associate you as the expert in herbalism. And, if you write intriguing romance stories, then your audience will identify you as an authority in romance writing. But, it's not enough for you to get the reader's attention; you must keep it beyond the confines of the online retailer. Otherwise, you are merely assisting the large online retailers with return customers. You need to implement a strategy to not only grow your audience but take them wherever you go.

GROW & MANAGE A FOLLOWING

I have bad news and good news. The negative side of self-publishing through any online retailer is you don't have customers, they do. After all, you may own the rights to your publications, but the online retailer is the one who dictates what you make and who buys your content. Yes, when the readers follow you and get all your books, you get paid. However, if the online retailers decide to change the rules on you—paying you fewer royalties, honoring bogus returns, or reporting fewer sales—then, you don't have much say. It's their platform; you're merely there to bring them business.

With a few strategies in place with each publication, you may end up on top. So, we know how to direct the traffic to your books, but how do we keep them? Here are a few examples of how to retain your audience through all your books:

1. **An Email List Sign-up** — Somewhere for your audience to opt-in for regular updates and notifications from you about your brand. Why make it hard for your readers to keep tabs on you? The email list is the best way to communicate with your fans and the easiest way for them to get your content.

2. **Relevant Social Media Links** — Most everyone is nose-deep in mobile devices and social media.

Meet them where they are and provide the easiest way to connect with you or your brand.

3. **About the Author** — Readers want to know they are reading books from a real person who they connect with on some kind of level. Don't take your author bio lightly, because this section is where they invest more interest in your brand.

You could grow and manage your following with just one of these factors—an email list. Because, even if you don't engage on social media platforms or keep an ambiguous writing presence, an email list is still the ideal way to keep your audience. Regardless of what the online retailers say, if you have a list of all your readers and a way to contact them, then you control your business. Without a list of your followers, you're still working for the online retailer.

Later, I'll cover email list building and a specific way to entice your audience to join your list. Also, I'll briefly touch on how you use an email list to build your business outside of the online retail platforms. In the meantime, shelf this topic, and we'll return to it momentarily.

CHAPTER 2
BUILDING AN EMAIL LIST

I won't make any grand illusion to being the consummate internet marketer. Though I've been in the publishing business for a little over six years, I am still relatively new to building an email list. But I know enough of the basics to have grown a few large email lists for various author brands. My audience retention is high; every book release subsequently gets greater purchase rates, and I've been able to provide my readers with much more than publications.

Furthermore, email lists aren't simply about making money, but more about keeping your audience and protecting the longevity of your business. But, you can't merely collect a bunch of emails and manage them in your regular email profile. Unfortunately, that method is unprofessional and leaves you susceptible to spam complaints and low reader retention. With the right email list management service, you handle your contacts better, tastefully keep your audience engaged, and retain more readers.

CHOOSING AN EMAIL LIST MANAGER

I could release an entire book on how to build and manage an email list, but we should stay on track with permafree books. The takeaway point is to authentically communicate with your audience on a regular basis. Send out, at least, one email per week at a consistent day and time. Ideally, deliver your email on a Tuesday, Wednesday, or Thursday for better open rates. Your messages shouldn't always be about selling. For instance, don't be afraid to ask what and how you could best provide what your audience wants.

Rest assured, if you use a reliable email list management service, then they will accommodate you with most of the information needed to manage your list effectively.

SUGGESTED SERVICES

When I started my self-publishing business, I didn't have much expense to spare. So, I used the free version of email list management services like MailChimp and

MailerLite. Admittedly, the multitude of features overwhelmed me. Now that I have a firm grasp of email marketing, the features make more sense. If you work on a tight budget, then MailChimp or MailerLite may be your best option.

The free MailChimp service has certain limitations that hinder your abilities to grow your audience. If you have a good grasp of doing intricate computer code (i.e. HTML, CSS), then you can get a bit more mileage out of it than I did. Otherwise, you are stuck with pretty plain features or a maze of confusing options. The biggest turn off to me is Mailchimp discourages affiliate offers and links, meaning you can only communicate with your audience and not sell them a single thing.

You get what you pay for in free email marketing services. Research other free email list management services but understand you will get the same value you invest. When you can afford it, look into upgrading or investing in premium services like Convertkit, Aweber, or the platform I use, SendFox.

USING THE EMAIL LIST

Your main goal of acquiring your reader's email is to retain customers no matter where you do business—online or off. Once your customers subscribe, you should provide them with an experience and not a sales presentation. Remember to build value, so give them relevant information in your niche or category. Think of your messages as making a friend, and it defuses this spammy, salesman-like approach commonly associated with email marketing. Here are five ways to communicate with your audience:

1. Share Relevant Information—any articles, personal insights, or anecdotes that support your primary niche.

2. Updates—create buzz and interest in upcoming book releases or appearances.

3. Unique Subscriber Deals—find ways to save them money on your books and even offer spots for advance readers/reviewers. Spoil them and make them feel part of something special or a members-only club.

4. Notifications—let them know when you have free promotions coming.

5. Affiliate Offers—establish an affiliate account with companies that offer products aligned with your niche. For example, if you are in diet and weight loss books, then you could provide affiliate links to diet products or subscriptions. Make sure you only endorse something you 100% approve. Otherwise, you diminish your chances of a trusting relationship with your subscribers.

Having an email management service is a necessity if you plan to release permafree books. Simply publishing free books to grow brand awareness is a poor investment of your time and money. Maximize the most from your exposure through permafree books—get an email list management service.

CHAPTER 3
THE IDEAL PERMAFREE BOOK

The best permafree book enhances your overall brand and complements your flagship book or main publication. For instance, my flagship book is The 90-Day Home Workout Plan, so I had to create spin-offs or related content. Permafree books on nutrition, targeted exercise programs, or cardio programs went great with my flagship.

Within each of my permafree books, I avoid repeating information featured in my flagship book. If I must share similar information, then I reword and abbreviate so I don't devalue the primary publication. Keeping my content brief builds more value in my flagship book and provides an incentive for people to purchase a copy.

IDEAL LENGTH OF PERMAFREE BOOK

How long you make your book is entirely up to you! A short read is perfect, but remember, build value, and don't simply release fluff. About 10,000 words or approximately 30 pages can be just enough. Research other books in your genre to determine an ideal length. Try to model successful books. Read reviews of other permafree books and find out what the readers like or dislike. Once you determine any missing factors or unwanted elements, fit into the gap the successful books have created.

THE IRRESISTIBLE OFFER TO OBTAIN AN EMAIL

Assuming you provide an exemplary permafree book filled with valuable content, your reader may want to opt-in to an email subscription. But, you should never lead your business based on assumptions. Additionally, your reader gets enough emails every day, so why would they want to get your email subscription?

Simply give your reader an offer they can't refuse—an irresistible deal or enticing offer. The incentive to join your subscription should be a one to fifteen-page report or short story relevant to your niche or brand. Obviously, what doesn't work is to offer a report on weight loss alternatives to an email list of avid romance readers. Conversely speaking, you may not have much success in giving a bundle of romance short stories to outdoor enthusiasts.

If you offer additional content, then you may further tempt them. Stick to short, yet sweet incentives that pack a punch and leave your readers craving more from you. Initially, start with one incentive and then gradually add more offers to entice your audience to part ways with their contact information.

Most email list management services store and deliver your incentive document to the appropriate subscribers. See your email list management service for details. If you are unable to get your service to host your report, then upload your file to a cloud drive. When someone opts into your list, provide them with the URL to download the report.

CHAPTER 4
THE BACK DOOR TO LARGE ONLINE RETAILERS

The only way Amazon will lower the price of a book to $0.00 is to make it available on alternative platforms for no cost. Once the alternative platforms distribute the free eBook to premium online retailers like Apple, Barnes & Noble, or Kobo, then Amazon will accommodate you. But, anything less than viable competitors, the online giant will scoff at the notion of a price match. Essentially, you need to publish on big online retailers to get Amazon's attention.

I've worked with two different alternative publishing platforms with great success—Smashwords and Draft2Digital. Either service provides the back-door entrance to Amazon's competitors, Apple, Barnes & Noble, and Kobo. I'd be remiss if I didn't mention these avenues offer much more than an opportunity for price matching. If you use these platforms wisely, then you can attract more readers and grow your audience faster. Don't take these smaller platforms for granted and simply use them for price matching at the online megastore, Amazon. I'll explain further with a review of both Smashwords and Draft2Digital.

1. Smashwords

    A. Pros: They have a wide array of online business partnerships known as their premium distribution, including the big online retailers of Apple, Barnes & Noble, and Kobo. Once you've uploaded your eBook, it takes about 48 hours for approval to premium channels. Then, in another 1-7 days, your book will appear in the Apple Books store, Barnes & Noble, and Kobo.

    B. Cons: Smashwords is a stickler for formatting and will not approve your book until you have met their rigidly specific guidelines. Once you learn how to format to their expectations, the process is rather simple. Also, they limit eBook file size to 10MB, which is not good for books with large picture files.

3. Draft2Digital (D2D)

   A. Pros: They have an easy book submission process and a smaller assortment of distribution partnerships, which include Apple, Barnes & Noble, and Kobo. They allow eBook files of up to 50MB, which is more than enough to accommodate most files. Also, D2D has a free interior formatting tool in their dashboard.

   B. Cons: If you have a picture-heavy ebook, it's going to be virtually impossible to use their interior formatting system while maintaining your layout.

I recommend using Draft2Digital because of its simple user interface and upload process. Rather than complicate an easy process, stick with a publishing platform who will have your best interests at heart. And, if you get stuck, Draft2Digital support is exemplary. If your sole purpose is to price match on Amazon, then either Smashwords or Draft2Digital will work.

GETTING AMAZON TO PRICE MATCH

First, you must publish the eBook to Kindle Direct Publishing (KDP). Do not opt into the KDP Select program since it requires an agreement to exclusive eBook distribution on Amazon for 90 days. Price your book a bit higher than normal, so customers have a higher perceived value of your price-matched book. Once Amazon honors your request to reduce your pricing, they'll put a line through the retail price and display the 100% savings. People love getting a bargain, so when they see your book has a considerable discount, they're less apt to refuse the excellent deal.

After your book goes live in the Amazon store, log into your KDP Dashboard, and scroll to the bottom of the page. Click on the *Contact Us* link. Then, you are given some options. Choose *Pricing*, then *Price Matching*. Fill in the details on the message. Be sure to include:

1. Name of your book & author

2. ASIN or Amazon product identifier

3. URL or link to your free book at Apple, Barnes & Noble, and Kobo

Don't bother sharing your bargain on small online retailers; Amazon won't price match on lesser competitors.

Amazon will notify you by email within 24-48 hours of your request. Most likely, they'll provide a canned response, such as:

1. We retain the discretion to pricing…we'll get back to you

2. We retain the discretion to pricing…and you'll find your free book at this link

The first option sucks because they never catch up with me about the price change. Most times, I discovered the book is free through my KDP Dashboard Reports. So, keep an eye on your book's product page if you get the former response.

GETTING AMAZON TO PRICE MATCH GLOBALLY

I discovered a neat trick that tripled my opt-in rate. Amazon is lazy when it comes to price matching. They'll only price match your book based on the region you publish. For instance, if you publish on .com, then they only price match on Amazon.com.

If you take the time to track your free book in every Apple region, then you can report your findings to Amazon and have them price match in those areas of the world. After you get distribution on Apple, here's how to find your book:

http://itunes.apple.com/**us**/book/isbn**9781310241451**

All you need to do is insert your book's ISBN after the "ISBN" in the URL. Then, after ".com/" you'll enter the region. For instance, here's how the link above would look for Canada:

http://itunes.apple.com/**ca**/book/isbn**9781310241451**

Repeat this process for all regions. The only area I have not been successful in price matching is India. Apparently, Apple, Barnes & Noble, and Kobo don't have eBook distribution in India.

Go through the same process in price matching, but mention every region all at once for the same ASIN. Keep Amazon accountable, because they were quick to shrug me off two times before I escalated my request. Persistence pays off. After two weeks of Amazon working on my price match request, every region marked my book down to free.

CHAPTER 5
FULLY UTILIZE YOUR FREE CONTENT

Once you make your content free, you should get the most mileage you can from it. Keep a spreadsheet of your permafree books, the links, and the publishing dates. Once every ninety days, submit your permafree book to free book promotion websites. Simply give your book information to these sites and choose one to five days as your supposed free book promotion days. If you look hard enough, then you'll find a few websites wanting your permafree books, too.

A while ago, I stumbled on a platform called NoiseTrade, a website devoted to free content. They provide their visitors with free music or eBooks in exchange for their email and an optional donation. I know a few authors who used NoiseTrade and invested in the promotional upgrades. One author had excellent results, acquiring a ton of emails and donations. The other author invested the same amount and only received a few dozen emails with little donations.

Personally, I don't mind donations for a free book. The reader could easily go to most any online retailer and get my book free, so the extra cash is nice. Nonetheless, I'm thankful they are willing to part ways with their email for my permafree book.

All you have to do to use NoiseTrade is upload your book like most other platforms. You'll need your book files in .pdf, .epub and .mobi. If you use Smashwords or Draft2Digital, simply download their converted files. Then, sit back and wait for the emails to come in.

After one month of having my permafree book on Noise-Trade, I collected 24 emails. That's exciting, considering I didn't have to pay a dime and gained a few more emails. So, since I found it worked, I uploaded the rest of my books. All I had to do was download and then upload their email spreadsheet to my list management service.

NoiseTrade offers only one author profile per login. So, if you are a self-publisher outsourcing your work, then you'd have to open numerous accounts to manage your different authors and permafree books. It's worth the time investment either way you shake it!

CONCLUSION

When I first started self-publishing, I thought it would be a simple business to manage and make profitable. Yet, I discovered putting out books isn't the same as making money for putting out books. When I learned how to produce quality publications and build a brand for long-term rewards, I started gaining momentum in my self-publishing pursuits. Rather than writing books as a hobby, I wrote valuable content to make an honest living.

Once I discovered the secrets of the permafree book, my business gradually grew. It wasn't an overnight success, but it came trickling in. First, I produced two permafree books and saw about one to four email subscribers per week. Then, I added four more permanently free books to my catalog, and I saw two things:

1. One new email subscriber per day

2. My sales drastically improved, increasing up to 30% each month

Then I added another two publications to my permafree collection, and the subscription rate moved up even more. Every week, I saw an increase in email subscribers and my front end sales. Once I started using my email list to build a back end business of affiliate products, another stream of income opened up. All this success happened within six months of my first permafree release.

Now, I'm confident my self-publishing business is still on an upward trajectory and here to stay. If you are new to publishing eBooks, then don't get overwhelmed. Take one step at a time. Find a good mentor or someone experienced and successful in self-publishing, so you increase your likelihood of victory. However, if you are a veteran in this business, then I'm certain you gained value in this book. Either way, use the steps shared in this book and you may see the same, if not better, results as I. Take care and good luck!

A SMALL ASK...

Now that you finished reading this book, what did you think of what you read? Were there any tips or information you found insightful? What do you think was missing from this book? While you're thinking back on what you read, it'd mean the world to me if you left an honest review on Amazon.

As you know, reviews play an integral part in building relevancy for all products. So, whether you found the information helpful or not, your candid review would help other customers make an informed purchase.

Also, based on your review, I'll adjust this publication and future editions. That way, you and other indie authors can learn and grow.

Feel free to leave a review at:

DaleLinks.com/ReviewPermafreeBook

ABOUT THE AUTHOR

Dale L. Roberts is a fitness author, video content creator, and self-publishing advocate. Voted by Feedspot among the Top 100 websites and Top 50 YouTube channels devoted to self-publishing, Dale has cemented his position as the go-to authority in the indie author community. Anyone who meets Dale for the first time will discover his enthusiasm and passion for business and life.

When Dale isn't publishing books, creating videos, and networking with business professionals, he loves to travel with his wife Kelli and spend time playing with his cat Izzie. He currently lives in Columbus, Ohio.

RELEVANT LINKS:

- Website - SelfPublishingWithDale.com
- YouTube – YouTube.com/SelfPublishingWithDale
- Twitter – Twitter.com/SelfPubWithDale
- Facebook - Facebook.com/SelfPubWithDale
- Instagram – Instagram.com/SelfPubWithDale
- DON'T GO HERE! – DaleLinks.com

BECOME A KEYWORD MASTER AND WATCH YOUR BOOK SALES GROW

If you can master keywords, then you can master your book's success! Dale L. Roberts is here to help you do that! In *Amazon Keywords for Books*, Dale shows you how to use keywords to sell more books. It's not difficult to increase the discoverability of your book. But you'll need a deeper understanding of keywords if you want to sell more books.

If you're ready to learn more and sell more through keyword mastery, then get your copy of *Amazon Keywords for Books* at…

DaleLinks.com/KeywordsBook

www.ingramcontent.com/pod-product-compliance
Lightning Source LLC
Chambersburg PA
CBHW060034040426
42333CB00042B/2451